P9-ECL-211

If We Knew Then What We Know Now...
We Wouldn't Be Us

ISBN: 978-1-68088-311-4

█ and Blue Mountain Press are registered in U.S. Patent and Trademark Office. Certain trademarks are used under license.

Printed in China.
First Printing: 2019

⊕ This book is printed on recycled paper.

This book is printed on paper that has been specially produced to be acid free (neutral pH) and contains no groundwood or unbleached pulp. It conforms with the requirements of the American National Standards Institute, Inc., so as to ensure that this book will last and be enjoyed by future generations.

Blue Mountain Arts, Inc.
P.O. Box 4549, Boulder, Colorado 80306

If We Knew Then What We Know Now...

We Wouldn't Be Us

Jo Renfro

Blue Mountain Press™
Boulder, Colorado

**Then we didn't always
stand up for what we believed in.**

Now we won't sit down
until we have our say.

Then we didn't want
to rock the boat.

Now we know that even if
we tip the boat over...
we can just start swimming.

Then we didn't want to grow up.

Now we know that growing up
means lots of adventures behind us
and more adventures to come.

Then we felt like we had to
compete with each other.

Now we know we are
stronger together.

Then we worried about
being by ourselves.

Now we value our time alone.

Then we were afraid to raise our
hands for fear of being wrong.

**Now we know that
no one is always right.**

Then we knew that we should be kind.

Now we know that being kind
can make the world a better place.

Then we didn't always try new things because we didn't want to look silly.

Now we try new things because
it's exciting. Who cares if
it looks silly!

Then we were always
comparing ourselves to others.

Now we embrace our differences.

Then we were afraid of falling.

Now we know we
can always get back up.

**Then we didn't always
speak our minds.**

**Now we know
our voices are worth hearing.**

**Then we didn't want to
listen to anyone else's ideas.**

Now we know that good ideas,
combined with other good ideas,
create great ideas.

Then we didn't laugh at ourselves.

**Now we laugh loud and often
because life is funny sometimes.**

Then we didn't always try
because we were afraid we'd fail.

**Now we know that not trying
is worse than failing.**

Then we didn't know
who we were.

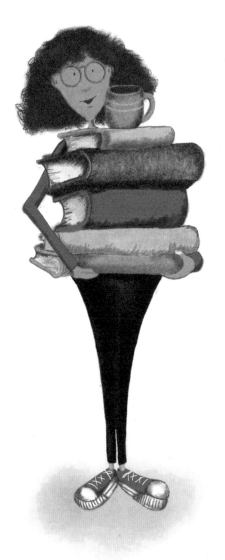

Now we know who we are, who
we want to be, and how to get there.

**Then we thought we had all
the time in the world.**

**Now we know that
time is precious.**

If we knew then
what we know now...
we wouldn't have
made mistakes
that we learned from
or spent time alone
getting to know
ourselves.

We might never have
spoken up, stood up, or
rocked the boat
to make a difference.
We wouldn't have
fallen down and
had to pull ourselves
back up to realize
how strong we are.

We wouldn't be us:

STRONG,
BOLD,
SMART,
GENUINE,
CONFIDENT,
KIND,
and
EMPATHETIC...

About the Author

Jo Renfro is a freelance writer and illustrator with a passion for mixing color, pattern, and whimsy in her somewhat quirky, often amusing, and always upbeat work.

She enjoys using her sense of humor developed from raising three kids, several dogs, numerous cats, and a potbellied pig named Matilda to create pieces that are lightheartedly inspirational.

Her love of the outdoors, animals, and her amazing kids are often reflected in her work.

A lifelong Kansan, she recently moved to Colorado to be close to the mountains, which still take her breath away every single day.